All that glitters

Wanderings & Wonderings of
a Changeling Bard

Halo Quin

All that glitters

© 2021 Halo Quin

The moral rights of the author have been asserted.

All rights reserved. No part of this publication may be reproduced, distributed, or transmitted in any form or by any means, including photocopying, recording, or other electronic or mechanical methods, without the prior written permission of the publisher, except in the case of brief quotations embodied in critical reviews and certain other non-commercial uses permitted by copyright law. For permission requests, write to the publisher at the email address below.

ISBN 978-1-9163396-5-1

HERBARY BOOKS

Published by Herbary Books
Caernarfon, Wales

www.herbarybooks.com
contact@herbarybooks.com

Contents

Dedication: To a Fairy Princess
1

Across the Veil
3

Looking for Faeries
5

Between the Thorns
9

Selkie
13

The Faerie Lover I - Silver Tongue
17

The Faerie Lover II - Tired on Sunday
19

The Changeling Child
23

Unwanted Attentions
27

Three Wishes
29

Faery Gold
31

Myths into Memories
33

Mother Holda, Keeper of Lost Children
37

Household Spirits I - Brownie
39

Household Spirits II - Hob
41

Will'O'Th'Wisp
45

The Kelpie I - Moonlit Beauty
47

The Kelpie II - A Good Meal
49

The Faery Harp
51

Birch Ghosts
55

The Thorns I - Whitethorn
57

The Thorns II - Blackthorn
59

The Dragons
63

The Faery Queen
67

Epilogue
71

Dedication:
To a Faery Princess

Once there was a princess faery,
with the deepest love of tales,
in her heart was carved a library,
where the stories safely dwelled.
Safely in her arms they snuggled,
knowing that she truly cared,
and knowing she would keep them always,
carried gently through the world.
Sometimes she would share her treasures,
with a loudmouthed goblin girl,
and they'd get to go a-dancing,
in the wide and verdant world.
But the stories loved their princess,
knowing she would keep them whole,
so they'd always come home quickly...
with another tale-friend in tow!

*For my fairytale Muse Leia,
the Good Folk, and their friends.*

Across the Veil

Sometimes you'll encounter,
little one,
a place where the air is thicker.
A space
where it pushes back against your hands,
little one,
a door waiting to be.

This book of charms is written for anyone who has felt that place where the air pushes back against your hands, where an unseen entrance to the otherworld awaits.

If you know it is possible, if you even suspect there might be a way to touch that magic, then this... this is for you.

In among the stories - my story, and their stories - are clues for how to find your way into faeryland and, if you're lucky, back again. Remember; the otherworld is home to both dreams and nightmares, so do be careful which horse you choose to ride.

Looking for Faeries

For glint of glitter in the air,
the flash of light that has no care,
for Tinkerbell and Barker's Fae
I'd search and search both night and day.

Deep in hedges, high in trees,
thorn-scratched palms and muddied knees,
never once a-wavering
I knew I'd find my Faery Kin.
I knew that Oberon was near,
I knew Titania's voice I'd hear,

I knew the whispers on the wind,
would delight and magic bring.
I held no thought of wishes three
nor gifts brought from the fae to me,
all I sought for hard and long,
was to learn that magic song,
just to feel enchantment's grace,
and magic's kiss upon this place.
I had no doubt that it was near,
and so I hunted with no fear.

Finally my wish was granted,
in my heart the knowledge planted,
underneath the old Yew-tree
their light arrived surrounding me.
I read them poems, sang them songs,
they took me to their realm 'ere long,
and I learned to walk the ways
'tween faery twilight and our days.

One word of warning I will share,
if you take magic in your care,
a changeling you will always be,
always betwixt and wandering.
Never home in either place
but blessed with sweetest faery grace,
one foot planted in each world,
whichever way they twist and turn...

Once they've caught you you are theirs,
and not all that glitters does play fair,
so if you choose enchantment's grace,
know there's a price that you must pay.
But even with that warning told,
I know now what they knew of old,
the cost indeed it may be high,
but with their blessing you will fly.
And once you've been there you will find,
you could not leave that bliss behind...

When I say I was obsessed, I mean it.

It was my Calling.

Every year from as early as I can remember, and even from before, if the stories are to be believed, I was *searching*. I could feel the magic in the world, just beyond what I was being told was reality. There was more going on, there were *secrets*. And the fair folk were the keepers. I knew they were there, I *knew* there were people hidden just out of sight and in the stories, the plays, the songs... all the words spelled out one enchantment: Faeries. Beings of magic and beauty, deeply connected to our world but just out of reach of the everyday. Our cousins. *My kin*.

I didn't quite fit in the world I saw, and there was more than the adults were letting on. So I was going to find the people who were going to share.

Looking back, there's no surprise that the truth was hidden from me as a child as the nature of magic is both beautiful and bloody. But I could feel it calling me, singing in my blood, whispering in the trees. There was wild and untamed enchantment and I was going to find it...

Between the Thorns

Do you see it?
That glimmer,
between the thorns?
Do you see it?
The glow that moves,
pirouetting across the green
between the veins?
Can you hear it?
That music just beyond,
just behind the ear?
Come.

Ducking beneath the bough,
fingers caught on rough, dark bark,
as we wriggle our way into the womb of the hedge,
the cave of thorns.
Beneath our feet,
earth slips,
slightly,
and we begin to fall.

It didn't take long for me to find others who felt the reality of magic, but it never took long for them to slip on the journey either. It's easier to accept the perspective that is thrust upon you every day, from every direction, over the music that whispers in your heart.

In fairness, perhaps it wasn't their song.

Regardless, that was their choice. This path isn't for everyone I suppose.

I could show them the shimmering, and they would show me in turn. We'd fumble our way between thorn trees and twilight and collect glittering moments to keep the guiding lantern lit. And then they would choose another path, often inviting me to follow them. Sometimes demanding that I validate their choice by choosing it myself. I lost friends when I said no.

I couldn't do otherwise.

The magic was always calling me. I thought I was pursuing it, but if that was true it was only because *it* chose to be pursued.

Selkie

Slipping my skin,
turning my toes,
on the beach where you found me,
gone.
I'll return,
only if you try
not to hold me too hard.
Do not keep me from the wild ocean waves.
Do not cage me,
in your narrow lives,
for I was made for dancing,
loving,
freedom,
under moonlit skies.
If you love me,
darling,
let me go.

The stories speak of *The Sight* like it's an obvious thing. For most of us that's not the case. Our visions of magic must be welcomed in, allowed to flow like the tides, turning, revealed by the moon's shifting faces. Like cherished dreams our memories fade under the pressure of the day-to-day which demands our attention and our obedience.

The selkie is a spirit who can shed their skin and move between the realm of the ocean and the realm of the land. In the water they appear as seals, and on the land they are beautiful dancers who entice mortals to fall in love. Their sealskins hold the magic which allows them to move between the worlds and it is said that lonely men would steal the skin of a beautiful selkie-maiden to make her their wife. She would always, eventually, retrieve her birthright and return to the waves. Before the tales of selkie-wives however, there were selkie-lovers, who would choose to take a human partner for a night, or a season, before returning to the water. Often they would leave beautiful, beloved, children in their wake.

Like the selkie, the touch of magic must be allowed to flow, invited to enter your life as a partner, not a prisoner. If you hold too tightly, grasping, it pines away. But if you become magic's lover... well, perhaps it will leave you with a gift.

The Faerie Lover I
Silver Tongue

come away, come away,
to my home evergreen,
come away in my arms
and see wonders unseen.

come away, come away,
and I'll make you a pledge,
you'll meet heaven on earth,
in my meadowsweet bed.

come away, come away,
let my long silver tongue,
tell you stories you'll swoon for,
come away, sweet one, come.

The kiss of enchantment is a blissful thing, a soaring sense of delight that pours through your soul, your flesh, and fills your crown to toe and beyond. Overflowing and expanding like you can spread your wings and escape all that holds you back, down, still. All while rooting you ever more deeply into your earthly body, reminding you what it is to be truly, wholly, vibrantly *alive*.

The Faerie Lover II
Tired on Sunday

I'll tell you a secret,
I know what they do,
before they yawn in my church,
and nap in my pews.
I know they've been courting,
with sweet faery men,
and I wish that they wouldn't,
I'm jealous of them!

In the pursuit of magic I was pulled this way
and that. So much of life needs attention.

There are meals to cook and chores to do and wages to earn and lessons to learn and people to love... The everyday sometimes feels like a jealous lover, it wants to keep me wrapped in its arms, to close my ears to the silvery song of the otherworld... But magic is always there, waiting. At night I'd slip out under the trees and sing to my beloveds. In the day I'd listen to the whispering wind and feel its gentle kiss upon my cheek.

The systems of the world are built to keep the wild in check. We are tamed by the structures that allow us to survive. But, even so... even so...

We witches know what it means to go feral. We know how to find that wildness in between the everyday and, once we do, it starts to seep in through the cracks. This is a commitment, something that takes time and devotion. Time spent listening to the trees is not time spent dusting the house. But what's a little dust when there's magic to be found instead? When we make magic a priority, we feed it in ourselves and in the world. And, sooner or later, even dusting can become a spell.

I built altars, shrines to magic, as an invitation for it to visit a while. In corners of my life at first, and then on every surface I could find. One took its place by the door so I'd remember the spirits at the edges of my home, be reminded of them as I stepped out into the world.

Sure enough, the more I allowed myself to dwell in the magic, the more it guided me.

The Changeling Child

One eye brown and one eye green,
cheekiest child that you've ever seen,
oak's ancient knowing held deep in those dreams,
strange for a small one, not quite as he seems.
Do not be wary, do not take fright,
if you care for him always he'll keep safe the night,
but if you would rather a meek child returned,
then fair's our exchange, so you'll lose what you've learned.

So things don't always turn out as we'd hoped, do they?

There's a tale from a century ago in Ireland of a husband so convinced his wife was a changeling that he held her in the fire in the hopes that, any moment now, the fairy lady that had taken her place would leave and return his obedient wife to him. She burned to death.

There are numerous folktales of strange, changeling children who were driven away by fire, or tricked into revealing themselves and sent back to faeryland through the lake. These stories tell us something true, and something horrific. People fear the strange. They fear that which they cannot control. They fear the wild magics and the unusual sense which rises with it. They turn away from it within themselves and their own lives.

What would you give up to be touched by magic? To find enchantment in your life? Would you accept the fear? Would you pay the price?

Some of us are born different anyway.

However hard we try to hide it, our oddness seeps through. We deviate from the standard and have to choose; close one eye forever and pretend they're both the same colour, or keep them wide open in challenge at the world. Not everyone even gets that choice.

I took tarot cards to school with me. Most people just found it quirky, but those that had always looked for an excuse to bully took this as permission to shut me out further. I turned to hiding in the library, painting visions, exploring possibilities between pages, and singing to the rain on my walks around the town. I had few friends, but I was always odd, always going to be odd. The price of keeping both eyes open was less than the blessings of the whispering forest.

It never occurred to me to turn back. And why should I?

Unwanted Attentions

Turn your coat now inside out,
to send their glance around you.
Hold an iron nail close,
to pin you to the ground.
Rowan hung above the door,
will keep their hounds at bay,
and blessed salt marks boundaries,
to send them on their way.
Wouldn't it be right and sweet
if this worked on mere mortals?
Seems like only Faery folk
behave just like they ought to.

In the stories and the voices of the spirits we not only find the path to magic, but also the rules by which to tread the otherworld. It didn't take much for my fellow travellers on the path of magic to turn away. A simply rejection and they admitted to the magic no more, and I believed them. Why would they lie? Why would anyone deny the possibilities?

And then I remember the changeling lady burned by her husband, and the jealousy of the people who seek to control the dreamers, to keep them small, and it makes sense somehow. A lie to keep the charade of normalcy. A lie to keep your magic hidden. A lie to keep you safe.

And then you begin to believe the lies you tell. And the spirits, listening, believe that you believe them. And so, why would they stay?

Truth becomes a strangeness in itself. And the strangeness loves the *True*.

Three Wishes

Each wish, a chance for better. Though all know the last must undo the first.

To enchant, we spell out the magic. We spell out reality.

Choose your words carefully, for words have power. Words shape reality. Words are wishes dropped into the well of the world.

True Thomas met the Faerie Queen on the riverbank under a Hawthorn tree. He served her well, and loved her better, in fair Elfland. In return she gave him the gift, or curse, of the tongue that cannot lie.

Ever after, all that he said, came true.

Was it true before he said it, or did his speaking make it so?

Faery Gold

Tell me,
when I pay you,
what will help you most?
Is it the gold you're asking for
or soil which is life's host?
Will the metal weighing heavy
in your pocket slow you down,
or keep you looking always
at what can be bought in town?
'cause I'm offering a secret,
which the old folk truly know,
that the most precious payment
is the earth where all things grow.

Once upon a time a farm-lad stumbled into the wrong market. He had some milk to sell and the tall fellow with the shoes of green gave him a gold coin, more money than the lad had ever seen before, and far more than the milk was worth.

When the boy left the market, laughing at his fortune, and the tall man's mistake, he slipped his hand into his pocket and found, where the gold coin had been, only leaves, dirt, and three tiny seeds.

What he did with them, well, that's anyone's guess.

Myths into Memories

Once we were gods, did you hear?
Once we were mighty and feared.
Once we were shining and bright,
now they call us tiny. They're right.

Once we strode proud and stood tall,
once we were well known by all,
now they've filled the world up so tight,
So we must be tiny, they're right.

Now our home seems so far to their minds,
where once we were neighbours in kind,
Now we're small in their stories and lives,
but we know how to glamour, you'll find.

They're right that we're tiny, but only for them,
only for those that forget we were friends.
Only for those that know not how to *See*
beyond mists of forgetting and into what's *Real*.

For we are the *Powers* that ever will ride,
beyond the everyday grind and despair of the tired.
We are the force of the wild and the gifts of the gods,
of the magic that weaves and the luck of the odds.

We slip in through the cracks of the tallest of tales,
we ride on the waves and the winds that still wail,
we weave gateways always and forever will,
for the promise that we recall still.

For your promise you'll recall us still.

It is said that when a seeker drinks from the Cauldron of Awen, the source of inspiration and magic, one of three things may happen.

They become dead, mad, or a poet.

It is said that magical gifts must be approached by one who is pure of heart, one who is honest and brave and true.

It is said that only the chosen of the spirits can drink and receive the gifts within.

Perhaps they are right.

Mother Holda, Keeper of Lost Children

Let me now hold you,
small child, lost one,
let me now hold you
your journey is done.
Let me now hold you,
small child, lost one,
in my home you are safe now,
far, far from harm.
Let me now hold you,
small child, lost one,
though your mother grieves you,
here you are home.

Good little children that fall down the well find themselves rewarded for their integrity. Mother Holda lives in the depths of winter, in a land on the other side of the water, waiting to catch them when they fall from a world that does not want them.

It is said that she looks after unbaptized babies too, those lost before the church can claim them.

There's a home for all unwanted children, with the Queen of the Winterlands. But be wary of her bright sister Perchta, as not all spirits are kind.

Household Spirits I
Brownie

Never quite seen
but always near
the brownie lives beside us.

A little dish
of cream sometimes
and she will always help us.

We share our home,
and must recall
that spirits long outlive us,

so heed her words,
mark her advice,
and hope she'll always bless us...

A list of suitable offerings:
- Milk or cream
- Honey
- Fresh, clean, water
- A dessert cooked just for them
- A place at the table
- A space in your home

Household Spirits II
Hob

Never forget a Faery,
Never them neglect,
Or what was once a helping hand
will turn straight to havoc.

Why's the world so crazy?
Why's its state so dire?
Have we lost the names of the brownies
who carefully tended our fires?

Have we forgotten giving,
thinking now only to take?
Have we forgotten the rules of the game,
realising only too late?

Hob stamps his foot in fury,
as the ocean is starting to rise,
and he's shaking our bones and our houses and hearts,
hoping we'll turn the tide.

Never forget the fae ones,
never them neglect,
or they who were once our family
will avenge the home we wrecked.

I have a theory.

My theory is that the Fair Folk are the powers of the wild, of nature, of cause and effect, made conscious. They are the magical spirits of those powers that rule our world.

Now, those processes and powers can be simple or complex, they have great range, certainly, and that is expressed in the many forms of the faerie people, however much like us they may appear. But when you read those stories, what happens?

There are rules. Rules of respect, of honouring the process, of keeping your word. There is cause, and effect.

If one is honourable and takes care of the land and the beings around you, the Good Folk usually treat one with fairness. But if one breaks a bargain, or shows entitlement, or makes an assumption about the stranger, then the punishment can be swift. Blessings are earned, and lost, on the integrity of one's heart, as seen through one's actions.

Just so, with Nature as a whole. The whole world operates on rules and humanity, as a species, survives through cooperation with each other and the land around us. If we are careless or take too much, sooner or later Nature, naturally, bites back...

Will'O'Th'Wisp

You're lucky.
There are those that would be grateful
for only a dip in
the icy lake.
You made it home,
in the end,
didn't you?

How well do you know the paths around your home? How well do you know the dangers? How easy would it be to lead you astray?

A word of caution, even for those who are kind of heart; not every light in the darkness is a warm fireplace or a torch held by friends to guide you home. If your gut tells you there's danger, watch that your feet aren't getting wet.

The Kelpie I
Moonlit Beauty

Beside the road there glimmered,
in the moonlight shimmered,
a glorious sight.

Eyes like pools of midnight,
coat of glistening starlight,
reflected on the sea.

The white horse stood there waiting,
a rider anticipating,
waiting there for me.

Beauteous beast so wild and free,
now bent down upon her knee,
so up I climbed.

Once settled safely on her back,
I felt the fear I'd lacked,
could this be...?

And sure enough I could not move,
as her racing it ensued,
into the sea.

I never stood a chance,
against this merry dance,
so I did drown.

Above the waves I float,
calling to the wandering boats,
"*Beware the mare!*

*For she'll lure you to her lair,
and feast upon you there,
and you'll never breathe clean air,
or live again.*"

Sometimes the most dangerous choices are
those that look the most delicious...

The Kelpie II
A Good Meal

It's funny how they think,
that they can take a horse to drink,
and we'll never need a good and hearty dinner.

When a rider I entice,
they think that I'll play nice,
but a Kelpie's got to get a good meal in her.

And it's only playing fair,
as they took fish from my lair,
that when I'm hungry I must find my meals on land.

So if you see a pony,
looking beautiful and lonely,
be a dear and have a glorious ride to sea.

'Cause it will be a joy,
as the world goes rushing by,
and you know you're doing your bit to help me.

There are two sides to every tale. Empathy, then, is a very useful tool for understanding what might be up ahead.

As is a decent guidebook.

And an ability to swim.

But death comes to us all in the end, wouldn't you rather experience the glorious world in all its beauty before you take that final trip to the underworld?

The Faery Harp

The voice of my sister
sings out to me.

She wishes she hadn't.

Too late now,
for the love of another
we all do things
we should not.

Strong fingers,
feel their way through my drowned bones
and golden locks,
long detached.
He weaves me together again.
Something in his eyes
tells me he is
entranced.
Good.
Then he shall do as I demand,
and I will not be silenced again.

We will visit my sister,
my bones become new,
my voice remade,
my song will haunt her,
for what she did to me.

As a harp I am reborn.
And when she hears the music
that I make,
she will join me, repenting,
and we will be sisters once more.
Beneath the water,
singing in harmony,
far from the realm of men.

Once upon a time were two friends who were close as sisters and who both loved the same man. One had fair hair and rosy cheeks and the other was pale with locks like a raven's wing against her neck. The young man fancied them both, but, loving either neither enough or both too much to choose, he decided to see how long he could get away with two maidens to warm his bed. Perhaps if he'd been honest, it would have turned out differently, but that was not to be.

He led them both along, telling each that she was his one and only, but that their love must be kept secret to protect her from his enemies.

For a while the darkness was his friend.

But truth has a way of coming home.

Golden-hair was kissing her lover on the jetty at high tide and the full moon sang in the dreams of her sister Raven-locks, waking her and calling her to the sea. There, as the waves kissed the wind and conjured foam, she heard her man playing lovebirds with another woman, face hidden in a deep hood.

She knew his voice, his laugh, the way his body moved.

Her heart broke and, in the blind rage that only pain can give rise to, she snuck up behind them and shoved them into the ocean where they were killed upon the rocks.

When her Golden sister did not appear the next day a sinking feeling in her belly began. Each day that passed it grew stronger, but she could not bring herself to admit what it might mean.

A year or two passed and a travelling harpist came to town. His harp was strange, made of ivory with golden strings. It sang so beautifully that everyone who heard it became entranced.

Raven-locks went to hear the musician play in the tavern that night. Of course, a magical instrument can sing its own song and, as it had every night since the musician had pulled the bones from the water, it sang of the sisters, their lover, and the sea. On hearing the haunting music Raven-locks' heart broke again, never to be mended.

Birch Ghosts

Thin white whisps,
wafting toward heaven,
beams of light
peeling
tree of beginnings,
birthings,
into this world
or the next?

What might it mean, do you think, that in the faery mound and the halls of the Otherworld a traveller is as likely to find an ancestor as a faery?

The Thorns I
Whitethorn

Sex scents the air,
when petals fall.
The Queen rides,
to find her lover,
to steal away
one who will grace her bower,
beneath the turning,
falling,
mayflower.
The immortal kiss of all-life meets
the limits of the flesh,

the thorns wrap themselves
round wrists,
held sweetly,
and draw a drop of blood,
or three,
to water the roots
of that which grows.

In the autumn,
those drops will blossom into haws.

The dance between the Fae and their human lovers highlights the symbiosis between magic and the sensual.

Enchantment is *felt* in the body.

Not a thought to be held, but pleasure to be filled by.

The Thorns II
Blackthorn

An old curse:
the thorn that carries poison.

May opens the way gently,
swooning,
but not this thorn.
Here the darkness bites
and sweet embrace
of scorned Queen
carries her lover deep into the night.

Intoxicated.

But if you look closely,
if you
pay attention
you see...
the thorn that bites the hardest
shares her beauty,
while the world
is still cold.

The thorns hold a gateway. On the one hand, Whitethorn, beautiful and giving. She lures us in with her gifts and her reminder that summer is here. Her magic opens the heart and soothes the weary traveller.

On the other hand, Blackthorn, whose thorns bite and whose scratch means infection. But the blackthorn blossoms first, bringing food to the pollinators early in the season, and she offers her dark fruit as the winter bites. One has to be tough to offer nourishment in the harshness.

Both have much to offer, despite the thorns. Or perhaps because of them.

It is no coincidence that they require

attention to the physical realm when you encounter them. If you wish to avoid their sharp bite then you have to remain aware of what they are, and what you are. Your soft hands reaching for their blessings. Your awareness sharpened by that kiss of risk and your spirits soothed by the beauty offered. In that moment, between risk and reward, flesh and spirit, pleasure and pain, you are focussed *Here*, at the crossroads of the *Now*. This is where all journeys begin. This is where the magic gets in.

Present. Open. Alive.

Here. Now.

Enchanted.

The Dragons

Wyrming deep beneath the earth,
lighting leylines like the hearth,
the dragons flow down deep within,
their power through the land they spin.

Riding high above the trees,
diving into caverns deep,
beneath the snow-capped, old mountain,
their power through the land they spin.

Sparking thought and starting fires,
warming hearts and lighting pyres,
forces far beyond our ken,
their power through the land they spin.

Walk the land with me.

Feel your feet on the earth which holds us.

Breathe deeply...
...and feel with your bones, your heart, your spirit.
... feel the dragons in the depths.

A long time ago a King was attempting to build a castle upon a hill. Whenever it was close to completion, the earth would shake and the tower would come tumbling down. He asked his advisors to help. Eventually they told him he needed to sacrifice a child with no father to break the curse that was keeping him from his desires.

A child with no father.

What an impossible ask.

And yet, one was found. It was said that his father was the Devil, or even, perhaps, the King of Faeryland himself. Whatever the truth of it, the boy was brought to the site and the king told him that his death would help bring a new age of peace to the land, and that he should be proud of his sacrifice.

The boy listened calmly and simply asked the king if his advisors knew about the dragons that slept beneath the mound that were shaking the foundations to pieces.

This knowledge saved his life.

That boy was Merlin. He knew about the dragons in the earth, the power of the land, the magic that flows through all things. When he grew up and became a great magician, where do you think his power came from?

The Faery Queen

From deep in the land rides Elfhame's fair Queen,
glowing with wonder and shining starlight,
for she is the magic of all that has been.

A mortal is blessed if her they have seen,
her song in their heart will fill them with light.
From deep in the land rides Elfhame's fair Queen.

Her human lovers keep the land evergreen,
and the touch of her blessing is bliss for a knight,
for she is the magic of all that has been.

But those that betray her will see her turn mean,
without full devotion, they are lost in her night.
From deep in the land rides Elfhame's fair Queen.

Ever present, all-weaving, of wonder and dream,
bridging the worlds with pathways so bright,
for she is the magic of all that has been.

So keep your eyes open and your vision keen,
your heart pure and true and your compass
set right.
From deep in the land rides Elfhame's fair Queen,
for she is the magic of all that has been.

Imagine, if you will, that you are on the bank
of a river, beneath a blossoming thorn tree.
The sun glitters on the surface of the water
and kisses your skin. You close your eyes
to feel its warmth more fully and hear the
rippling of the river singing like the chiming
of beautiful bells.

The bells grow louder and you feel a
presence. Your eyes open and before you
sits a heavenly lady in shimmering green
upon a tall, white horse. The air is thick with
magic and the scent of blossom, like she

is all around you and this fine lady is only a fragment of the swirling power made visible. The water breathes with her. The tree branches wave with her movements. The land pulses with a heartbeat that you somehow know is hers.

If she offered you her hand, if she offered to guide you to the otherworld and show you sights beyond your wildest dreams, would you say *yes*?

If she offered you a piece of that magic, so that you could carry it into the human realm, to keep it alive, would you say *yes*?

If she offered you a kiss, the love of the otherworld, with all that entails… would you say *yes*?

The vision fades, but you can hear the bells in the distance still.

Epilogue

Slowly as the wheel turns,
as the sun at solstice burns,
as the riotous thorn-tree blooms,
enchantment fills the land.

Slowly as the cities grow,
as the lamps steal sunlight's glow,
as the books begin to know,
enchantment fills the land.

Slowly as our lives wear on,
as childhood dreams have upped and gone,
though work and chores now fill the home,
enchantment fills the land,
and faerie, ever nearer draws,
between the grey and tired sighs,
with spark of colour, sharp delight,
draws closer to hand...
... as enchantment fills the land.

Anyone who tells you that magic is dead is either lying or a fool. Anyone who tells you it will be an easy path, however, is just as bad.

The truth lies somewhere in between. In the caress of the wind and the blessing of the thorns. In the beauty of a poem and the walking of the land. In the touch of the mysteries when you live them yourself.

Here is a key, and the start of a map.

Your heart is your compass.

The song of faerie, your guide.

Good luck.

WITH A LOVE FOR BOOKS

With a large range of imprints, from herbal medicine, self-sufficiency, physical and mental wellbeing, food, memoirs and many more, Herbary Books is shaped by the passion for writing and bringing innovative ideas close to our readers.

All our authors put their hearts into their books and as publishers we just lend a helping hand to bring their creation to life.

Thank you to our authors and to you, dear reader.

Discover and purchase all our books on
WWW.HERBARYBOOKS.COM

www.ingramcontent.com/pod-product-compliance
Lightning Source LLC
Chambersburg PA
CBHW031546080526
44588CB00018B/2717